A More Human Face

Other Books by Donna Brook

Poetry

A History of the Afghan
Notes on Space/Time
What Being Responsible Means to Me

For Young Readers

The Journey of English (nonfiction)

A More Human Face

Donna Brook

Hanging Loose Press
Brooklyn, New York

Published by Hanging Loose Press, 231 Wyckoff Street, Brooklyn, NY 11217-2208.

Printed in the United States of America
10 9 8 7 6 5 4 3 2 1

Thanks to *Hanging Loose, Flatiron, River Styx, Transfer, Verse* and *The World*, where some of these pieces originally appeared. *Spontaneous Combustion* was printed as a broadside by The Alternative Press of Ann Arbor, Michigan.

Many poems within are dedicated to individuals who have given me much needed personal and professional support and encouragement, but the editors of Hanging Loose Press, most especially the steadfast Robert Hershon, deserve more thanks than I know how to give, as do my family and friends, who "know who you are."

Hanging Loose Press thanks the Literature Program of the New York State Council on the Arts for a grant in support of the publication of this book.

Cover art by Ann Mikolowski
Cover design by Caroline Drabik

Library of Congress Cataloging-in-Publication Data
Brook, Donna
    A more human face / Donna Brook.
        p.   cm.
    ISBN 1-882413-59-8. -- ISBN 1-882413-58-X (pbk.)
    I. Title.
PS3552.R657M67   1998
811'.54--dc21   98-41803
                                                              CIP

Produced at The Print Center, Inc., 225 Varick St., New York, NY 10014, a non-profit facility for literary and arts-related publications. (212) 206-8465

Contents

for Ken and Ann Mikolowski

*That other world that was the world
is no longer the world.*

Nadine Gordimer

Am I a Poet?

*...There should be
so much more, not of orange, of
words, of how terrible orange is
and life.*

Frank O'Hara

I never mention azure skies. I don't
know what color azure is
but maybe real poets do, or they
could just like how it sounds
instead of baby or royal or light or navy
or periwinkle.
I assure you. I azure you,
my darling.

My friend, who is 74 years into a writing life, kept company with
Williams and Oppen and Reznikoff and, recently, told a lady his
Selected Poems was being published simultaneously in both Britain
and America. She said, "Oh, is this your first book?"

Nobody asks a self-proclaimed dentist if he's ever pulled a tooth.
Nobody asks the greengrocer his credentials for appraising arugula.
Everybody always says to the poet, "Published?"

In my case, yes.
The Magna Carta,
"We'll Never Forget You Big Vinny" on a wall on 3rd St.
between 1st & 2nd Avenues,
the lyrics for Motown classics,
everything that confounds assembly.

This morning, my what-may-be-possibly-poems
throw ashes on my head and tear my clothing,
at lunch, go berserk over world stupidity,

and, later, at twilight, pose a Hidatsa-Hadassah profile
against the orange sky.

The sky
inside a blood orange
on a windy day
up a winding road
as they rowed
toward the azure shore.

An Afternoon in Suffolk

Because Timothy is eighteen months older than Andrew, he remembers Disneyland better and is more excited about the Americans. He walks purposefully beside his father on the platform until the couple appears, then runs ahead with Andrew — disdainful, aware, leading the way home.

Huburt and Alice, arriving with the girls, honk into the drive, and soon everyone is talking at once. Timothy escapes to his bedroom and brings down his magic set. He runs his hands over the familiar, smooth, frayed, glossy, large rectangle, the top of the box. He removes the cover and takes a quick inventory: the cling wand, the interlocking rings, the dot card, the magic coin box, cups and balls, the shell trick. Timothy reaches for his deck of marked cards.

The American woman picks a card. The American man picks a card. The woman chooses again — a different trick — and then the man. "That's enough, Timothy," his father says. Andrew picks cards and Timothy names their locations in the deck three times. Then they change places, and it is Timothy's turn to pick while Andrew is magician. The four of diamonds. The nine of clubs. Andrew names the bottom card correctly four times. Then Timothy deals a royal flush, and they are soothed, engrossed, separate. They know they do this very well.

Then everyone must go to the pub.

Here the strangers are glaringly obvious. Where will so many of them sit? What will the girls get to drink? What kind of crisps? It is a weekend afternoon, and Timothy sees other children he knows in the pub, but he does not let them past the metallic gleam, the hard bright colors of the Americans. He is lucky and does not get a seat so he must lean against his mother's legs. In some part of his mind, a filly nuzzles her foal, maybe a real horse, maybe a greeting card.

At the beach, things are more relaxed. The adults stop talking and everybody kicks a football. Timothy is glad of his lungs and the giant North Sea at his back. Now he can run; Andrew and their parents can run. Only the Americans do not run but go for a walk.

At one point, the American woman is a far turquoise dot against the differing grays of sky, water and sand. The old ladies of Felixstowe totter in and out of their line of weathered-wood dressing cottages. Huburt runs past Andrew. Andrew runs past Timothy. Alice kicks the ball.

Back at the house, Timothy's mother puts out meats and salads. Afterwards, Alice and Huburt and the girls go home. His father decides to drive the Americans to the train in Ipswich and run some errands for his mother. Timothy is already wearing his corduroy bedroom slippers, but, fortunately, no one notices. Now is his chance.

His father and the American man sit in the front while Timothy is paired in back with the woman. They speed faster and faster to make the train. As his father leans over the wheel, Timothy tenses his own shoulders and lightly punches the woman in the forearm.

"Hey," she says evenly. "You know, I'm fifth-grade homeroom teacher, and no one hits me, ever."

Timothy and the woman are caught and waiting for several seconds as the tiny car flies through the fields at dusk.

"What's the principal crop around here?" the American woman casually asks Timothy.

"Mustard," he politely replies.

April 27, 1994

for Mary and Frank Ferrari

Evidently she can't hear me
bellow "Dinner!" so I climb
two flights of stairs and knock
on Martin Luther King's nose.

"From every mountainside,
let freedom ring!"

I push open the door past Malcolm X

"The future belongs to those
who prepare for it today."

and bend over under Steve Biko.

"We have set out on a quest for true humanity, and somewhere on
the distant horizon we can see the glittering prize. Let us march
forth with courage and determination, drawing strength from our
common plight and our brotherhood. In time we shall be in a posi-
tion to bestow upon South Africa the greatest gift possible — a
more human face."

This face is fast asleep.

"Dinner!" I yell at it. "It's time to eat dinner!"

    ✿

"You say no.
Time says yes.
Free South Africa.
April 27, 1994,"
says my T-shirt.

What do people say
with their forefingers?

"One Settler. One Bullet."
"One Person. One Vote."

One relevant piece of information:
by the year 2056,
a minority of United States citizens
will be descended from Europeans
while the majority's heritage
will be African, Asian, Central, Native
and South American.

What idea
speeds from their index digits as they
pull down their opposable thumbs?

     ✿

"Mandla"

In Zulu, it means "Power."
In Yiddish, it means "soup nuts."

Building a Staircase by Hand

for Sherman Alexie

In our Brooklyn backyard, a Mexican
craftsman sits for days
sanding spindles. "In the U.S.," he says,
"people have no respect for the wood."
Hell
people
don't even respect each other
let alone trees,
and when I ask him why
there's one leftover step
leaning against a wall,
Crescencio
disses the lowly slab of pine.
"Oh, that piece.
He wasn't good enough
for the stairs. I'll make
some other thing."

❀

The Barnes & Noble on Fifth Avenue and Eighteenth Street
shelves novelists like Leslie Silko under *Indian* not *Fiction
Alphabetical by Author,* so James Welch is kept with
Crazy Horse, who never even published so much as
one collection of short stories with a university press.

❀

Alice comes back from her recent trip to South Africa affirming
that the blacks still hate the Indians more verbally than they do the
whites. She means, of course, the other kind of Indians, not the
ones here and in Latin America. The Indians from India who were
born in South Africa.

＊

It isn't easy
building a staircase by hand but
it's worth it we all agree
as Bob and Nombuyi and I go
up and down in our daily living
first careful about loose or missing
steps then changing position as we cross
from the part that's still the old
wobbly slant to the new firm wood;
it's so damn beautiful it should be a table
this staircase and when Crescencio
begins the second staircase
we talk to him through the spaces
where the risers have been; he's
in the basement smiling out at us
and we're in the front hall waving
playfully at him.

The Cure

for Jack Anderson and George Dorris

we are having a pleasant dinner in a quiet
Thai restaurant and I don't think Jack is even
listening to the conversation but admiring the tank of
red and orange tropical fish when he says that
in the Fifties
some schools of psychiatry claimed all
a gay man needed to get cured was sex
with an aggressive woman
even just once
have
I got a girl friend for you Jack she's the best
of Madonna
Ethel Merman
and Alex Karras of course
I don't know what you'd do about the over
thirty years of love and tenderness George has
devoted to you
but you'd be cured

and probably out of a job and life's work
since you wouldn't want to write reviews of guys
in tights or poems but you'd
be normal one
of the studs saying
lie down bitch
and let me stick it to you

it was a late spring weekend night
such as this some years ago
when we four were crossing the street
in the Village and a New Jersey driver
almost ran George down get out of my way

you old faggot he yelled and there was so
much hate in his voice I nearly threw up
while my husband went wild and reverted four decades
to a spasm of high-school locker-room rage
lunging halfway through the car
window shaking the man by the shoulders screaming
the most damning insult his teenage brain knew
shut up you lousy cocksucker leave him alone

Diagnostics

The minutiae of other people's lives may appear to be seen only under the microscope and yet any wriggling detail can be the substance. If someone says, "I'm a diabetic," the listener automatically thinks of injections, usually ignorant of the daily adjustments and computations of diet, schedule, fluids. "Listen you moron," the disabled, disadvantaged, handicapped person wants to scream, "this is how I live. This is what I do all the time."

"Do you," asks the doctor, "keep rechecking to see if you've set the alarm clock or constantly make sure you have your keys?"

"Yes."

Now the doctor knows you have some degree of panic disorder, obsessive-compulsive behavior or agoraphobia.

"Do you wash your hands repeatedly until they bleed?"

Let me give you this example. A young Haitian came to teach French at a fancy private girls' school. On Parents' Night, when she shook hands with one of the fathers, he immediately ran his right palm down the leg of his pants, as if he had been sweating. She didn't come back to the school the next year. But that was just part of it, of course. Part of the notation on the pertinent, focus on the relevant, hitting the nail on the head. Bingo. You may want to know why the man did that, consciously or unconsciously, and the point that involved me was how the woman viewed it. Maybe the man had an obsessive-compulsive disorder and feared germs from any contact. Maybe he sometimes washed his hands repeatedly till they bled.

So then, there is the superficial and glaringly obvious First Level, such as a man without arms or the only Sikh in the room, but there is a vaster, almost infinite Second Level: people on renal dialysis; people with colostomies, mastectomies, and pacemakers; ex-convicts; reformed manic-depressives; former nuns and priests. I know one woman whose father was Rumanian and whose mother was Japanese and another woman whose mother was Chinese and father Australian, so they both had to check the box "Other."

Finally, there is this illustration of a woman who had a phobia about taking elevators alone. She was okay if other people were in the elevator but could not stand to be shut in by herself. When she moved to a city heavily dependent on elevators, she struggled to overcome her fear and was successful, but she found that her behavior in an otherwise uninhabited elevator was impeccable, as if all the eyes in the world were trained on her.

When she could have farted or danced, she behaved exceptionally maturely, grasping, clawing toward normality through her shame.

A Dog Wearing Wallpaper

When I say I overslept she says
"Don't you have an alarm clock?" "No," I
want to answer real snotty, "we use a rooster."

And when I tell Bob she asked if we
had an alarm clock, he says, "Tell her,
'No. We keep chickens.'" That's the joke

enthralled in my marriage a shared hatred
of anything on the walls but white paint and art,
mutual amusement at cats. Oh but don't

let a wet springer spaniel
jump all over us licking our pink cheeks!
The love in a life

includes this absence
of repeating cabbage roses
these lingering barnyard smells.

The Editor's Alphabet and Couplets

in honor of Dick Lourie

I

after-hours
aftertaste

daydreaming
dimwit

eye-catching
firebomb

gaping
get-up

heavy-handed
hit man

interracial
know-how

lighthearted
Mafia (cap)

no-holds-barred
pickup truck

postcard
roadhouse

savvy
shortcomings

so-called
sunglasses

upside down
wish fulfillment

II

The prefix "co" is not followed by a hyphen but in "co-worker"
it is according to the *OED* to avoid saying "cow-orker"

which one rarely does. A person can't be commemorated
till after death. All clicks
are audible. Very few women, even older ones, wear
panties under pajama bottoms but who knows. I

am sure that:

> short-order cooks do not wear tuxedos (see p. 21),
> the phrase "feathers and beads" does not sound fierce per se
> (34),
> a five-year-old is usually smaller than a ten-year-old (40).

It probably takes more than a few months
to destroy a T-shirt (97).

Sociopaths are not necessarily
childhood bedwetters (119-120).

III

change red
to blue (9 & 81)

change shirt
to dress (900)

change twice a day to twice a week
change on a daily basis to twice a day (6,130)

change happy
to acting happy

change a dirty bookstore to either
a porno bookstore or a store that sells dirty books change

Cain and Abel
to David and Goliath

omit "The memory rumbles his stomach" add
"But, no cockroaches" for emphasis

Florida Power and Light

for Bob; for Barbara Hershon 1909-1995

I wonder how, when my death comes, I'll act.
If anger, jealousy and lies will eat
my cells or if I'll settle for the fact
and let my matter turn back into heat,

my one for all and all for one, in peace.
I hope my ego will not want my name
emblazoned on the heavens, that release
into all earth, air, water, fire, will claim

no phony dignity or extra hour.
Time counts ... and then don't add up to a hill
of beans. We all aspire to Florida Power
and Light, but, in the end, the tubes that fill

the corridors of wallpaper take hold.
I want an honest end when I grow cold.

For Alex

The first time I saw my great-nephew the doctors
had completely paralyzed all three pounds
of him to cease
his painful agitation in his Plexiglas box.

like a prince in amber
a doll in aspic
ripped untimely from his mother's womb

a neonate's suspended animation

"Five more minutes, just five more minutes," said the surgeon,
"and we would have lost them both."

The first time I saw my great-nephew the wires
to moving zigzags, mysterious blinkings and beeps
obscured the tiny Pampers with the decorated waistband
as days before my niece's eyes had rolled
above the respirator, the wraps for hypothermia, the blood
right from the fridge like a carton of cow's milk

like a calf's bad dream

like eating lead paint
like scrawny limbs, bloated stomach, copper hair
and rickets
infants addicted, toddlers abused
teenagers tortured
oxygen deprived

"When will we be sure there's been no permanent damage," asks
my exasperated father. *"Probably not in your lifetime,"* I answer.
"We're all to some degree damaged in one way or other,"
the listening psychologist says.

The first time I saw my great-nephew he had problems,
a black and white panda bear, apnea,
a minuscule stocking cap, and feeding tubes in his nose.
He'd already cost hundreds of thousands of dollars.

Save the Children
(or the Whales or the Forests
Our Cities)

Save Alex

Who cares
if this is or is not a good poem?
Who cares what my intellect said
about quality of life?
Now, this is *my* family.

The first time I saw my great-nephew I saw
grandmas and grandpas and daddies and mommies in Infant
ICU on the sixth floor, while up on the tenth floor, the healthy
happy babies were displayed through the glass as they waited
to go home to Harlem
or else to the Upper East Side.

"For No Clear Reason"

When I was safe I was scared
because of serotonin. Nobody
even knew it was there so how
can you blame them? It was all
in my synapses all the time
and now it has all gone away with just
80 mgs of good medicine and 2 mgs
of getting it right.

Feeling better than I've ever felt before
even nighttimes alone in the big house
sleeping with bars on the windows, not, of course,
to keep me in but them out.
Car with The Club on the ignition, special locks
on the doors, trunk, steering wheel. Stolen (twice),
every window smashed like Kristallnacht.
But just annoying, infuriating, pain
in the ass. At least I think that's where
I feel the bite. It's not like
trying to get health insurance.

What does it take now to terrify?

Manhattan Bridge
hasn't fallen down, yet.
But there's always
the subway fire stabbing crash unlicensed driver
and tap water, the possibility
of bubonic plague
from hormones in the milk.

(Every day a city
props up its metal with timber
burned by the homeless for warmth
every night.)

In grades K through eight, public school students will be allowed
to get TB but not lunch, pregnant
but not literate in high school.
We will continue to encourage them all
to turn white.

I dreamt last night
the fright was over.

But the new fright had begun.

Hard Rain

for Eric J. Cassell, M.D.

Someday that boy will be a man
staring out his bedroom window during a March storm
saying to his wife in the bed without turning
his eyes away from the downpour, "It
was a night just like this
when my mother died," and she
will know what not to answer
opening the soft dark wet of her body
to grief and its opposite

Like me
rousing my husband as I do now at two a.m. and giving
my whole flesh over to his hands
I become as deep and real as earth in rain
and then he enters me

So, in one home a patient is dead
and in another a patient is finally claiming living, and
elsewhere, down a different street
in yet another borough, a sleeper
scratches his innocent arm
and does not dream.

I Have My James Schuyler Too

Just because I lived in Detroit for 22 years doesn't make me
without memories or feelings and once John Ashbery
was in my charge when I was a graduate student, nobody
else was available to see he got lunch and from Macomb County
Community College to his evening reading, so it was just me and
    John
Ashbery eating in Warren, Michigan. He told me how
he had to have minor surgery and asked how much I thought
it would hurt and, of course, I only wanted
to hear what it was like to *know* Frank O'Hara.

All of today I've been wondering why I always thought
this particular woman you've probably never heard of
lives in Chelsea, and then tonight at the reading
for *The Diary of James Schuyler* at the Poetry Project,
in New York City, where I've now lived for 18 years,
I remembered my son had said she lived on 23rd Street,
so, of course, I must have kept imagining the Chelsea Hotel,
the only reason I ever seem to think about 23rd Street,
just as James Schuyler is the only reason
I ever think about flowers.

In 1974 or so John Ashbery
walked in through my parents' front door
and out the back to their garage
so I could drive him to Wayne State University,
and the following Sunday my mother looked at a big picture
of him in *The New York Times Book Review* and said
to me with astonishment and almost a hint of accusation,
"This man walked through my kitchen!"

I suppose that's more or less
my mother's John Ashbery, and I have
my James Schuyler too.

In Fact

for Paul Violi

Actually even if
the British German second-rate art scholars
in Florentine restaurants don't
like vulgar opinionated American women, I do.
I am one,
and I was glad that you understood
how I actually understand actually
although maybe it's a cheap thrill when so few people
actually understand *you.*
Thank you
anyway.
Anyway I have to go
to sleep now so I can get up early and order
children around the Dewey Decimal System.
March them up to the card catalogs and make them yodel
call numbers. 811 is still
one of my favorites, where
you really are, actually.
Actually
don't be flattered by this dedication
as I'm not playing favorites
but you fit best
into this particular poem.

Message to Mary Ferrari in Jo'burg

The typesetter had changed "Gelato" to "Zealot"
so your stanza began:

"TWO ARMIES FACE EACH OTHER
ACROSS THE ARABIAN DESERT
I wish they were in Rome with us eating dessert.
Zealot Mixed is a good dessert
if you have accidentally ordered
a fish's head first."

How I wish
the world was in the Piazza Navona eating *tartufo* but
when the Europeans first met the Khoikhoi at the Cape
it was not "a warm or promising encounter"

the indigenous people
ate offal and lice, smeared
themselves with grease and cow dung, draped
"the entrails of grass-eating animals
around their necks and legs,
as decoration and as portable delicacy."

So it was no *nocciola*
when ignorant cultures clashed on sight,

"Practically everything about the Khoikhoi gave offence," although
"Much of this can seem surprising, considering the conditions from
which so many sailors and soldiers disembarked; the stench of the
places in which they themselves slept and ate on board, the filth of
their own unwashed bodies."

Do you think urbanity will desert us?

Do you think I will be able to provide a good home
for this Xhosa teenager to whom I have already given
delicacies she'd never heard of before:
jam, cherries, shrimp, salami, books about the Sioux?

(When Nombuyiselo arrived in America and somebody promised
to take her to Disney World, she said, "Mouse? What mouse? I have
no history with this mouse.")

Thank God you're a Catholic
when we need all the prayers we can get. We need
ubuntu, and scholarships. We must say,
Umntu ngumntu ngabantu
every night before we go to sleep:

*People
are people
through other people.*

Or they are inexplicable; some
circumcising prep school graduates with sticks; others giving
SATS to kids who were never shown where Italy is on the globe.

Are we sure this thing is round?

Just meet me at Vivoli —
you know, near Santa Croce — or better
yet right in the Pazzi Chapel and we'll have *semifreddo*
afterwards. I'll show you
the sterling silver bracelet Bob gave me, each
link is a different face from a fountain in Rome.

Where you are it is wintertime
and dinner time. Here
in the August lunch hour of eastern U.S.A.
people are still awaiting
their just desserts.
Zealots on ice.

Summer, 1993

34

Moonlight Bingo at Saint Leo the Great

for my father

My father has decided to play, or just
watch the moonlit players
during a snowstorm in Buffalo, New York.

It is always snowing,
and my father
has driven through the cold midnight and stinging
crystals to see for himself
how the *goyim* have fun
in spite of December,
its silver and visible air.
My father wants
more air.
His lungs are freezing
as he waits
for the game to begin or maybe
for the game to be over. You can never
tell with my father,
whose lungs are icing up
while the numbers are whispered out
at Saint Leo's.

Usually,
a person is made an official saint
because he
or she
stopped doing something awful
or, more usually, came
to regret it afterward,
when it no longer appealed.
Then shouldn't my father
become a saint

because now he's sorry
that he smoked? The air
looks like smoke
coming out of a cold mouth
in a cold place.
Just before
my father's mother
died at age 97 only a few
months ago, she held tightly
to a small piece of paper that read:
"IOU 25 CENTS."
"Bingo," she gasped
out to
my mother, one of
the last things my grandmother said.

My father in-
hales
and exhales
after climbing
the flight of pearly stairs
to the moon
where the saints all live
over Buffalo, New York.

My First Encounter with the Natives
of the Pacific Northwest

for Maureen Owen,
and in memory of Robert Eaglestaff

I.

At Seattle's Indian Heritage School a teacher says,
"There were 14 in my reservation
high school graduating class in 1972 and I'm the only one
left alive. I've been the only one
for ten years."

II.

The Indians give us dried sage.
They hold a salmon feast
in our honor.
They present us with a Navaho blanket
and a video tape.

III.

Those kids in the preschool who have fetal alcohol
syndrome can't focus on group poems, but a girl from
the bright-eyed group tells us, "A very sad thing is
a monkey who only has one arm. He can't swing
and eat a banana at the same time."

IV.

When we show up at his aunt's house
on the Lummi Reservation, they call down to Matt,
the shy flute player, "There's three people
here for you. An old woman, an old man
and an Indian."

V.

Here is a Seattle postcard of locks and a fish ladder,
Drive Thru Espresso, the Cascades, The Market, but also
the pigeons, drunks and crows. Lots
and lots of crows
who are eating up the songbirds.

The New York Hospital Poem

> *Sun*
> *on the river*
> *flashing past*

> *James Schuyler*

I. Twilight

Ten hours after surgery
I look out through the haze
to see a tall silhouette
from the back.
The creature's arms are raised to the heavens
as are, I presume, its eyes, its fingers spread.
It's Eric
in a dark suit
fiddling with the curtains
around the bed. I am
greatly relieved and disappointed.
I thought it was The Devil
or a big bat.

II. Protocol

I always feel that if I had been an important functionary
in the court of the Dowager Empress right before
the Boxer Rebellion I would understand teaching hospitals.

Full-fledged male doctors stand at the foot of the bed
and give some sort of signal when they're going to move in.
"Let's have a look at that wound."

Female residents and interns come close up to my right side
and make excellent eye contact, looking
exceptionally clean with very healthy hair.

But then this is a few days' limited survey based on six people
and takes into account only gender, age and who bills.
It is thrown off by Dr. Simonson,

the resident with baby-blue eyes, who often
stands to the left of my pillow so that all I can watch
is the female intern listening to him talk to me.

III. Drugs

Every three and one half hours
I ask for that shot
of morphine
and get it.

Even out of it
I know I'm in
the upper middle class because
the nurse reassures me, "Whenever
you need your
medication
just say so."

IV. My Great Secret Terror Revealed

This long corridor is all gynecological surgery and
high-risk pregnancies so some patients lumber by
stroking their unborn hopes and some drag along
holding in their emptiness. Emmett
worries that I will go into a depression
because any possibility of pregnancy is totally gone.

The desire to bear a child
died in me completely, Em, when I was nine years old
so strong was my fear
of passing on to a baby
whatever was wrong with me.

40

V. Urine

"Aren't hospitals funny places," says Dr. T. with the usual
reference to bottoms hanging out.
But it's the reverence for excretion I like.
People measuring urine. People carefully pouring urine
from one container to another as if testing out Piaget. People
carrying their own urine around with them in bags, and the nurse
wants to look into the toilet bowl before you flush.
She compliments me on my quiet stoicism
during the enema and I am amazed by how
the other women carry on. How odd
to find your waste so socially acceptable.
It's like the best memories of toilet training.

The interest. The applause.

VI. The Woman Whose Bed is Kitty-Corner from Mine

seems nice but dumb.
She fascinates and repels me.
All her company is family
and she has many large loud
relatives who all enter by saying
"I love you" and depart
by saying "I love you"
while the top-volume in-between
conversation is full of hostility,
suspicion and backbiting.

I have memorized the history
of this woman's undiagnosed pain
and the tests done or to be done.
Why haven't her sons and sisters and
cousins and nieces? Or have they?
And the minute her daughters leave,
she calls her grandchildren on the phone

and says, "Hello. Grandma loves you.
Good-bye. Grandma loves you."

VII. Let Me Out

I'm really in a state
after being up all night very
sick to my stomach having had
a set-to with the nurses and my
doctor's stupid service calls him
after I asked her to have him call me
after he called in so the nurse is ticked
at me for getting her in trouble with
the doctor who is annoyed at me for waking
him up so that by the time he comes
in hours later I answer him with the
petulance of the spoiled child
I've always been
honeybunched and hugged all my life
for my cute comic cleverness,

oh, I wish my hair hadn't just been tonsured
so I could suck on the end of a braid!

VIII. Scars

My brother is a favorite visitor
because he looks so well and happy
and happy that I am getting well. It was
almost twenty-one years ago that it took forty-five minutes
a day to change the dressing on his mangled hand, and now
you can't even tell which fingers move and which
don't unless you know. My husband
is jealous that my new scar is so neat when his
stomach looks like it was put back together by
monkeys or accident in 1957. Three a.m.

and I watch the traffic move on the Drive, the water
rush past

the scars in my father's heart
the line across my mother's throat
my brother's cockeyed index finger

Yes, yes. We all know how time is like the East River,
and we are grateful that, at the moment, we're alive.

Parent as a Verb

In Pathmark, I run into this acquaintance/neighbor/peripheral person who says to me in hushed tones what is so often said to me in hushed tones and always makes me angry.

"You're so good at mothering. It's too bad you never had kids of your own."

Now I'm not exactly alone here. Within the range of my bellow are fifteen-year-old Thandi, who needs ginger beer and coconut cookies, and thirteen-year-old Matthew, who needs soda and ranch-flavored chips, and eleven-year-old Jesse, who needs whatever I won't buy. Not to mention the shadowy troops of middle school students past and present and the future readers of my children's books. Lady, I've got kids. Or to be more precise, I've got interest in kids like money in the bank and joy of kids like pennies from heaven. What I do not have is past pregnancy.

So I reply to the "kids of my own" as I always reply.

"Haven't you heard about Lincoln's Emancipation Proclamation? You're not supposed to own anyone."

So I seem the rude bitch, don't I? But something is required to balance this other view of me as so good I run around requisitioning children. Yes, Thandi's parents returned to Durban and left her with us so she could get a better education, and she's only on loan, and yes, I had the bad form to become a stepmother, but I didn't kill the woman. She died of all too natural causes and, OK, I prefer to teach ten-year-olds over college and high school students, but I have my reasons, and I don't have a heart of gold. I don't even have any more time to explain this because I've got three kids wandering around a supermarket.

While you may have heard that it takes a whole village to raise a child, or however that goes, it actually takes a whole society, and the recognition that childhood is a stage through which everybody passes, and never quite leaves entirely. *They* don't get cranky when they are sleepy or hungry. *We* do. Don't get me started.

When I was eight years old, I saw a TV documentary about a family composed of children adopted from all over the place. One of those a-dozen-at-dinner families. I became an adoption fanatic. I'd sit in the back seat looking at the rain and streetlights as my father drove through the dark, and I'd list to myself all the wonders I'd share with my new formerly poor and lonely sibling. I was besotted. Obsessed. When my parents felt no pressing need for more than the two children they already had, I resolved that when I got to be a grown-up.... But by the time I grew up, I wasn't any family service's ideal, and I'd learned the costs of college and dentist, discovered the limits of time and self-determination. So, I meandered into parenting as previously discussed.

Now, I use parent as a verb because my friend Nell told me that, somewhere, Anna Freud wrote that the person who does the parenting is the parent. The word caretaker enjoys a current vogue in terms of children, but it reminds me of someone who trims hedges on English estates, and caregiver isn't right either because children require a lot more than care. Thought helps. Patience comes in handy. I mean, this is about people who, if they don't lose or destroy them, outgrow their shoes in months that seem like minutes. Let's pay some attention to detail.

So, if I buy the only plastic tray of coconut wafers on the shelf — jumbo enormous — Thandi cannot possibly eat a worthy percentage of them before she as usual abandons them to a state soggy or stale. Ditto huge plastic go-flat-immediately bottles of Pepsi versus cans and any overpriced box of cereal that contains Dayglo pebbles. I am wavering between budgetary concerns and whining. Maybe the problem is that I haven't accumulated enough children for modern packaging methods, or enough children who'll all eat the same things. Kids are out there waiting to be collected like trash at the curb, God knows. And if not picked up, they will be beaten or sexually assaulted or taken to Disney animations. All worse than my caving into junk food cravings when, on rare occasions, I do not shop alone.

Alone is what's easier. With can become surrounded-fraught-with-guilt. Are there others like me who so carefully avoided bringing one more soul into this world of forgotten souls, who got a package deal in marriage and liked it that way, who admit that they don't feel that they've missed out on an essential by never giving birth but would hate a life lived always and only in one's own age group?

Motives are never clean or unconfused. I've missed out and gotten freebies. Probably, to drag in that doctor and poet, nobody's driving the car. Or pushing the cart. But we are proceeding toward checkout.

People Don't Die Just So You Can Write a Poem about Them

The night after Bradley shot himself
Ken and I started arguing about
how old he had been. "Bradley is,"
I said, "the same age as I am
or younger."

But of course there was as always
in these cases all that talent, a shoe,
Detroit, intelligence, orange, humor,
scarlet tongues and magenta crowd scenes
of goons and plumbing parts —

So, Bradley Jones, (1944 till Yesterday),
now I am about to be
older than another dead person.

Poem Found on Parents' Night

for Kate Mellon

I said

This is an age
where you need to allow her more
freedom
more risk-taking
or you might create
an unnecessary struggle.

Her mother replied

I had a dream
where Kenya told me
she was moving to France
and I said
You can't move to France.
You're only nine years old.
But she did
and I followed her.
When I got there
she was already all set up.
She'd gotten some French parents
to adopt her
and she'd changed her name
to Mozambique.

Reading

The famous writer, mentioned often as a Nobel Prize contender or at least a must-read, went into the ladies' room and raised her graying hair off her neck in a gesture famous from Balthus. Were there any signs of perspiration on her pink oversized shirt she asked the mirror on the wall? Did the garment fall smoothly or cling indecorously to bra or buttocks? A woman who writes so much and so well of the body surely must live in it. This body, so tiny and compact, made it seem as if the famous writer had plotted to be small, to emphasize her thrust through her diminutive stature. How wonderful that such enormous intelligent books should issue from such a nymph. It would have been a slight victory over sexism if the very observation had not been sexist.

The famous writer dropped her arms and tilted her head, delighting in the smooth fall of hair. She had been smart to wait until New York to get it cut, for now, with this blunt cut and this silk shirt, these tapered black slacks and smart shoes, she did not look like a famous writer. She looked like — I don't know — like 850 Park Avenue or 12 Fifth Avenue or Central Park West around 79th Street. She looked like a doctor's wife, except in the facial expression, in the eyes. It was another victory over the stereotypical and another nail driven into her isolation as the famous writer folded sections of her hair over her hand. She reminded herself that the fluorescence of ladies' rooms makes everyone look sickly and that in America the serious writer remains incognito. You can go any day in America and see Norman Mailer walking around Brooklyn Heights in sweatpants. The famous writer dropped her hairbrush into her purse. Right now, she wasn't interested in Norman Mailer in sweatpants but in automatic pilot and hypnotic trance.

For this was not going to be a college reading or an old-friends-show-up-unexpectedly reading. This was the kind of reading where some people came to have books signed, listening to her voice only to increase the cash value of their copies. Some came just to gaze at her as if she were a sacred relic. Others had bought a series subscription and had never read a thing she'd written. So, there was no leeway here of youth or provincialism. Before the reading, there would be an announcement that she would only sign three volumes per person, and, after the reading, she would stand at the head of a coiling snake, signing her name and signing her name. She was no longer flustered by this experience, only distanced down a road of self, and as for the thought that she had been mistaken for Saint Theresa, well ... as anyone finds out who has ever been the center of attention for even a moment, as a bride or at a Bar Mitzvah or slipping on a crowded staircase, even giving a speech of whatever length or sort — being a shining star means giving the power to the observer; the source of strength is not the one who's being looked *at* after all. Only skill, of language, of presentation, can wrest control of the situation and make the attraction something other than the Mona Lisa, the Pieta, the thing. This requires real work, and so cannot be the swept-away thrill of ego except in fantasies. If all the people are looking at you, you must give them something, do something, or you will become the something they take away from the night.

Now the famous writer was introduced by the well-known head of the well-regarded writing program, and she began to read a recent story. From long practice, she stood so that she would not sway or be blocked by the podium, looked up from her book at appropriate intervals, modulated her voice, and gave herself over to her words. And here was where everything fell into place. For she really was an excellent writer, and her language carried her as it carried those who actually listened, blurring those definitions writer and reader as the writer read her writing and the reader became the listener as the barmaid in Manet's famous painting is only paint, and should be looking at a gentleman, but looks straight at you. The famous writer read with political commitment and years of accumulated rage against injustice, wanting to sway her audience to action, injunction, embargo, effect. She read with the soft moans of her favorite vowels pleasing her and the open collar of her silk shirt standing away from her throat. She read with relief that now, for these moments while she read, she was distracted from her son's final grade in a required statistics course, from her distance from home and husband, from aging. Instead, the woman in the story spoke and moved, listened to the husband in the story, cared for the child, and ultimately fell from grace. The auditorium applauded, and the famous writer gave a few small bashful nods, almost and in place of bows.

Next came the questions the famous author had agreed to answer a few of.

"Where do you get the ideas for your stories?"

"What writers have influenced you the most?"

"When did you realize that you had such exceptional talent?"

"What is the difference between a long short story and a short novel or novella?"

"How did you first get published?"

Then the well-known head of the well-regarded writing program, who was fielding questions for the famous writer, called on a young woman in the third row. And the young woman stood, face flushing, and asked a question, a real question.

Immediately, the famous writer realized by the question that the young woman had read a great deal of her work and had understood it. Furthermore, the young woman appeared to grasp the political climate surrounding the author and to know the implications of what she asked. It would have required at least half an hour to cover the question adequately, perhaps more, and it was the kind of question usually asked by a favored graduate student at a party or by an interviewer with a tape recorder in a hotel room, maybe not even then. It was certainly out of place here. (The young woman had probably asked it because she had no other place or person to ask. She seemed to really wish to know.) And all action stopped as the two people on the stage pivoted toward the short figure in the audience. Come to think of it, thought the famous writer, it was a very perceptive, telling question, the kind one's ideal reader would ask. It made one curious about the person who would ask it, and the writer looked at her interrogator thoroughly.

"That's an interesting question," said the famous writer. "But I really couldn't say."

Robert Hershon at Home and Abroad

The first time he was in Italy my husband
always checked to see how many museum
guards had crossword puzzle books and now in Paris
he keeps asking me questions about the gutters.
Who turns on the water? Who turns off
the water? What are all those rags for and who
put them there do they direct the flow
of the water? Who are those guys in bright green
with bright green plastic brooms that
used to belong to Victor Hugo? Robert Hershon
wants to know, and he also wants to sing
"Negro spirituals" translated into Italian
from a book he bought in Milan, and hum,
and drum his fingers, and whisper the lines
of poems to himself as he types them. We are
driving to Silver Spring, Maryland, and my husband
is telling me how Miles Davis found Charlie Parker
exasperating. Miles says, says my husband, that
he was in a taxi with Parker, trying to tell him
something but Bird had his girlfriend going
down on him, a quart of bourbon in one hand and
a whole roast chicken in the other. It's such a
wonderful picture of excess, Bob says.

Second Marriage

I.

Once there was something minor
called an avalanche
that fell of its own weight to bury all
the movement of your heart.

Snow melts. Spring comes.
Eleven years since you bought those dark blue sheets
with the white floral pattern. You went to meet a plane
from Minnesota by mistake while I dis-
embarked the aircraft from Detroit
to shower you with shoes

and brown rice.

II.

I wince whenever you say,
"My first wife," as if this were
a horse race and I will always be
runner-up. Can't you say,
"My late wife," "my former wife," "my marriage
that turned into ash"?
Mother of your children.
Companion of your youth.
In your poem, you lift her flannel nightgown.
In my life, there has never been anyone else
I was married to.

III.

Hated bourgeois bondage doublethink.
I chew at the ropes of wedlock that bind me to the mast,

but the hemp is double-knotted like a first-grader's sneakers.
Marriage clips one's mittens to one's cuffs
as the safety of the ultimate grown-up
commitment:
  "a pledge or a promise"
  "confinement to a mental institution."
Double talk pillow talk and punt.

IV.

The famous orange cat died
because we couldn't stand his misery and his replacement
now licks his black paws at my feet. "I never,"
you said the other night, "thought I would care for this
new cat as much as I do." And we let this cat
sleep with us.

Spontaneous Combustion

for Larry Zirlin

I think of this not
as metaphor or image
but incident
phenomenon where persons
burn to a crisp for no apparent reason
at temperatures of about 3,000 degrees
Fahrenheit leaving
a pile of ashes
oily residue and
occasionally
an unburnt limb
nothing
around the victim is damaged
except perhaps the exact spot
where the deceased ignited,

but as I said, it's not a symbol
it's an occurrence
such as you probably remember
from Chapter 32 of *Bleak House*
Dickens found thirty cases on record
and today there are more than
200 reported cases of spontaneous
human combustion, which can
happen to anybody
at any time

Twenty-two-year old Marilee Mars
was laughing and joking in the shower
after gym class when smoke
started pouring out of her ears and
mouth and then she caught fire

as cold water poured down on her
she burned intensely for about 10 minutes

but not from lust
deep-seated psychological problems
conflicts
alcoholism
deposits of flammable body fat
phosphorous
or sin

these were or have been proposed
as explanations
when:

Luis Ponce exploded while performing an exorcism in Barcelona;
Christian Ruys and his fiancee, Patrice, burst into flames in a shop-
ping mall in Brussels; Paul Lemers erupted while waiting in a
crowded line to buy theater tickets in Vienna; Dr. J. Irving Bentley
of Couldersport, PA, was discovered by a meter reader on Decem-
ber 5, 1966. Dr. Bentley apparently ignited while he was in the
bathroom and burned a two-and-a-half-by-three-foot hole through
the flooring, with only a portion of one leg remaining intact.
Nearby paint was unscorched.

I know you are wondering what
I am getting at you
are the kind of person who thinks
that because this is a poem
there is some meaning
if you must have a meaning
this is what I mean

children at summer camp
like to lie on their backs
gazing at the stars they are enthralled

56

by the ancient Egyptian process
of mummification where the brain
was removed through the nostrils
for the big chunks
the ancient Egyptians
crushed the back of the skull
and used a spoon

Tell the Truth

for Molly Frances

just because no one really knows
what is memory what forgery what
's in a name
that was changed from Morris
to Maurice to Mark how
old anybody is

truth is a justly famous metaphor
as in she was frightened by an alligator
belt
logo
probably plastic anyway
or a crocodile

if you can't tell the difference
it might not be any different
is this a school of Van Dyke
beard does a breast
implant create a real breast
is a Jew made up of culture

race religion conversion or style
I have come to see you
as a red-headed college graduate
named Molly Frances
love
is a highly regarded metaphor too

Theories of My Childhood

I believe that one of my most important childhood theories was my Development of Language Model. The primary conceptual work for the Language Model was done when I was approximately four years of age. I am still proud of the scientific thought process used in my formulation. Observing my great-grandmother, father's parents, father, and younger brother gave me the largest cross-reference available to me at that time. First, I noted that the human animal does not have any language when born. I further observed that it slowly develops the ability to understand and then to speak English. I saw that a human can, by young adulthood, understand but not yet speak Yiddish. By mid-life, both Yiddish and English are spoken and understood, but by old age, English has disappeared and only Yiddish is available for communication. It is true that I abandoned this explanation when I began formal schooling, and that my study lacked a control group and a wide enough data base, but my resources were limited at that juncture.

During this same time period, I made some unfortunate assumptions about the procreation of the species. Having heard and, I believed, understood the Daddy Plants the Seed Hypothesis, I became emotionally overwrought when my father purchased, and presented me with, a set of miniature garden tools — rake, etc. — for my new sandbox. I remember postulating that I was much too inexperienced to be responsible for a child as I was myself a child, and painfully aware of it. Since I felt an unexplainable revulsion about divulging my concerns, it is possible that my parents still wonder about what must have been to them my inexplicable reaction. Refer to the work of Freud et al.

Other conceptualizations from my early life have fallen away with the years: (1) my conviction that, given the opportunity, people respond with empathy; (2) my idea that inhibition is simply a formality observed for the sake of convention; (3) my notion that prejudice comes from nonacquaintance. Over the decades, I have, unhappily, become convinced that there are individuals who will not tell someone who has to take pills on the hour what time it is. Many a woman has never been seen wearing less than a flannel nightie. There is probably a man in, for purposes of illustration, Los Angeles, who counts 5,420 people of various colors, beliefs and sexual orientations as his close friends, but observes that "they're exceptions" and "not like the rest of them." Yet I cherish to this day a construct of my single-digit existence — that is, that affirming change is possible, and all change inevitable. This ideation seems essential to all my postulates. Why, right at this very moment in time, as I stand before you encased in human vulnerability, I can look down and see my chubby little fist closed tightly around something of such value that my grip can only be described by the metaphor "iron." I conjecture that I will never see my palm again for, if I open my hand, hope will have melted.

Waiting

At the times in life while waiting for life
to happen it's a pleasure
just to fall down stairs
for the thumping and bounce.

It's why to throw alarm clocks
across the room at mirrors out the window
or work radical changes on hair and self-esteem.
Right now
excuses are forming for naps,
the letter is almost ready that reads, "we regret
we are pleased to inform you
that we are happy to say we are sorry to tell
you no yes yes no."
Or else not.

Sure once everything happened
at high speeds and bright orange
right between my legs
in kilometers and Spandex.

Now this is all for me alone
in my sweet English cottage
of pity and washed-out pastels.

What Normal Women Consider

*Nevertheless, it is difficult to conceive of a normal woman
who would consider tipping a masseur 45 cents for the
favor of masturbating her to orgasm.*
                    The New Sex Therapy

Whatever class I was in in Kenmore, New York, there were
always two Jews, me
and somebody else, but the other person was always a practicing
Jew and my father was a socialist
during the Eisenhower Presidency
and added to that I had a number of phobias and
unexpected ideas, for instance

once my family was at a party for Norman Thomas during the
period when I knew God looked just like him, very tall with white
hair and the skin stretched so tight across the bones of his face, and
somebody said, "Here is Gene's girl," and Norman Thomas put his
hand on my shoulder, and I thought these words exactly: "He is just
like Jesus suffering the little children to come unto him," even
though I knew that that was a very bad thought.

I have also done bad deeds
because I did not know I wasn't supposed to,
and my best friend screamed at me and screamed at me
while we were making tomato sauce to freeze for her mother,
"What do you mean you swallow it! You mean you
swallow it?" And she was waving a wooden spoon.

So here I am abnormal to this day,
and worse a poet,
but suddenly happy
lying on the clean towel, the steel table, the
Japanese boy with the short square fingers
serving me

green tea and myself.

Yes, a freak like me has paid a lot of dues
but some days my oyster is the world
twice for less than a buck.

WIPPSI

the never-changing wet mess of birth, of coupling, living
in this hamster-on-its-wheel metropolis because of heterosexual
    love
with a new cruel knowledge of family life each secret
hanging in the window of a Chinese restaurant like a duck,
and this ... this man
who rubs Avocado Body Lotion into my back
comes home, reaches into the ice cubes,
pours the Scotch, doesn't seem to know
what the hell I do for a living

"Michael," he tells me, "had to go to a special testing center for
standardized tests that all the private schools require for kinder-
garten. Isn't that amazing?" "No."

many, many Monday afternoons of
looking at scores on an overhead projector plus
a month of workshops describing each subtest
of the WIPPSI in detail also
every year I give a full set of ERBs to ten-year-olds who
cry each year if a child's
performance on the Vocabulary Subtest is at
great variance with her score on the Comprehension we assume
she is experiencing a high level of anxiety but if another little girl
at another school arrives dirty and covered with bruises nobody
    seems
to assume a damn thing

Suppose, when he was working on Animal House, Michael tried to
fit the sheep into the cow space? Suppose he got lost in Mazes,
dizzy in Geometric Design, inappropriate during Vocabulary?
What if in Picture Completion he finally painted that space Gilbert
Stuart left around Washington? What if, in Similarities, he said that

the Elizabethans called orgasm dying because he'd heard that at home? Yet Arithmetic would never be a problem. Everyone in New York City knows what adds up. I teach what adds up to those who added up well. And if, in the Information Subtest, when he was asked, "What do you need if it rains," Michael said, "an umbrella," he'd be judged fine but average. If he said, "a big boat with two of every kind of animal," no one would know if he were well-informed or terrified. These tests are not easy to interpret. People must be trained to administer and decipher them. The scores do not have visible results like black-and-blue marks.

maybe it's because it's sentimental Xmastime
that I'm so aware of who is a child and who shouldn't be
but all that rain-forest August
Charles and Paula wouldn't close their bedroom door
to run the air-conditioning unit
so that they could hear Michael sleep

Notes

The quotation from Nadine Gordimer is from *Writing and Being: The Charles Eliot Norton Lectures, 1994,* published by Harvard University Press in 1995.

"For No Clear Reason" is the title of a poem by Robert Creeley. I quote from his poem in mine.

The quotations in "Message to Mary Ferrari in Jo'burg" are from Noel Mostert's book *Frontiers: The Epic of South Africa's Creation and the Tragedy of the Xhosa People,* published in the U.S. by Knopf in 1992. In his *The Mind of South Africa,* published by Knopf in 1990, Allister Sparks writes about the meaning of *ubuntu* and the phrase "People are people through other people." Further explanations and translation of this important concept were provided to me by Lulama and Nombuyiselo Ntshingwa.

The anecdote about Miles Davis and Charlie Parker is told in *Miles: The Autobiography* by Miles Davis and Quincy Troupe.

The initials WIPPSI stand for Wechsler Preschool and Primary Scale of Intelligence.